WORLD WAR I

Remembering the Great War

WORLD WAR I: THE CAUSE FOR WAR

NATALIE HYDE

 Crabtree Publishing Company

www.crabtreebooks.com

WORLD WAR I
Remembering
the Great War

Author: Natalie Hyde
Editor: Lynn Peppas
Proofreader: Lisa Slone, Wendy Scavuzzo
Editorial director: Kathy Middleton
Production coordinator: Shivi Sharma
Design: Margaret Amy Salter
Cover design: Ken Wright
Photo research: Nivisha Sinha,
    Crystal Sikkens
Maps: Contentra Technologies
**Production coordinator and
    Prepress technician:** Tammy McGarr
Print coordinator: Katharine Berti

Written, developed, and produced by
Contentra Technologies

Cover: Assassination of Franz Ferdinand
and his wife Sophie, June 28, 1914
Title page: Wilhelm II, Kaiser of
Germany, during the manoeuvres
of 1905
Contents page: The Proclamation of
Wilhelm I as Kaiser of Germany, in
the Hall of Mirrors at Versailles on
January 18, 1871

Photo Credits:
Alamy: 9 (© Image Asset Management Ltd), 11t (© Military Images), 11bl (© akg-
    images), 12–13 (© INTERFOTO), 21 (© akg-images), 24 (© INTERFOTO),
    25 (© INTERFOTO), 27 (© akg-images), 30 (© liszt collection)
The Bridgeman Art Library: 20 (A meeting of the three finance ministers of the Triple
    Entente (b/w photo), French Photographer, (20th century)/Private Collection/
    © Look and Learn/Elgar Collection), 39 (German reserve soldiers leaving for the
    Western Front, Berlin, 1914 (b/w photo), Haeckel, Georg (1873–1942) and
    Haeckel, Otto (1872–1945)/© SZ Photo / Scherl)
Corbis: 29 (© Bettmann)
Getty Images: Content Page (The Bridgeman Art Library), 4 (Lee Ergulec), 5 (Hulton
    Archive), 8 (Hulton Royals Collection), 10 (The Bridgeman Art Library),
    18 (De Agostini), 32 (Universal Images Group), 37 (De Agostini Picture Library),
    38 (UIG via Getty Images), 42 (Hulton Archive), 44 (Popperfoto)
© Imperial War Museums (INS 6062): 26
India Picture: 14 (De Agostini Picture Library), 15 (Mary), 16 (Heritage Images),
    17 (Everett), 34 (De Agostini Picture Library), 35 (Mary)
Library of Congress: 22 (LC-B2- 3258-11), 40–41 (LC-USZ62-136086)
Oliver-Bonjoch: 13br
Shutterstock.com: 11br (Netfalls-Remy Musser)
U.S. Defenseimagery.mil: 23
Walters Art Museum: 19
Cover: Private Collection / ©Bianchetti/Leemage / The Bridgeman Art Library
Back cover: Wikimedia Commons: Library and Archives Canada (background)
    Shutterstock: I. Pilon (medals); Shuttertock: IanC66 (airplane)
Title page: © Imperial War Museums (HU 68473)

t=Top, bl=Bottom Left, br=Bottom Right

Library and Archives Canada Cataloguing in Publication

Hyde, Natalie, 1963-, author
    World War I : the cause of war / Natalie Hyde.

(World War I : remembering the Great War)
Includes index.
Issued in print and electronic formats.
ISBN 978-0-7787-0387-7 (bound).--ISBN 978-0-7787-0393-8 (pbk.).--
ISBN 978-1-4271-7505-2 (pdf).--ISBN 978-1-4271-7499-4 (html)

    1. World War, 1914-1918--Causes--Juvenile literature. I. Title.
II. Title: World War One. III. Title: World War 1.

D511.H93 2014   j940.3'11   C2014-903225-0
                                          C2014-903226-9

Library of Congress Cataloging-in-Publication Data

Hyde, Natalie, 1963-
  World War I : the cause for war / Natalie Hyde.
      pages cm. -- (World War I : remembering the Great War)
  Includes index.
  Audience: Ages 10-13.
  ISBN 978-0-7787-0387-7 (library binding : alk. paper) --
ISBN 978-0-7787-0393-8 (pbk. : alk. paper) -- ISBN 978-1-4271-7505-2
(electronic pdf) -- ISBN 978-1-4271-7499-4 (electronic html)
  1. World War, 1914-1918--Causes--Juvenile literature. I. Title.

D511.H94 2014
940.3'11--dc23
                                          2014017796

Crabtree Publishing Company

www.crabtreebooks.com   1-800-387-7650

Printed in Canada/052014/MA20140505

Published in Canada
Crabtree Publishing
616 Welland Ave.
St. Catharines, Ontario
L2M 5V6

Published in the United States
Crabtree Publishing
PMB 59051
350 Fifth Avenue, 59th Floor
New York, New York 10118

Published in the United Kingdom
Crabtree Publishing
Maritime House
Basin Road North, Hove
BN41 1WR

Published in Australia
Crabtree Publishing
3 Charles Street
Coburg North
VIC, 3058

CONTENTS

THE WAR TO END ALL WARS

ABOVE: *This French national cemetery contains the graves of 15,000 soldiers who perished during World War I.*

World War I was known as "The Great War" and "The War to End All Wars." It was truly a global war. It was the first time in history that so many nations and people had been involved in a conflict. Over 65 million men from 30 different countries took part. Almost 8 million soldiers and 4 million civilians would die in four years of fighting from 1914 to 1918.

World War I would also be very different from any war the world had seen before. It was the first war to use airplanes and tanks. Troops also used long-range **artillery**, flamethrowers, barbed wire, and poisonous gas. Before 1914, soldiers on horseback, called cavalry, had been a powerful fighting force. Now, they were virtually useless against these advanced weapons. Massive battles took place with hundreds of thousands of soldiers on each side. New and deadly weapons changed the way battles were fought. Trench warfare replaced field battles. Soldiers lived in these trenches for months. Lines of trenches of enemy soldiers with machine guns were separated by **no-man's land**.

CHANGES IN EUROPE

The cause of such a large and devastating war cannot be traced back to one event. Europe in the last half of the 19th century was dealing with many changes. The five Great Powers of Europe were Britain, France, Russia, Germany, and Austria-Hungary. They raced to protect and expand their empires. The **Ottoman Empire** in southern Europe was falling apart. Many people in this region wanted their independence. Nations formed **alliances**. These agreements were made so that nations would support each other if war should occur.

The lives of ordinary people were also changing. This was due, in large part, to a new age of steam power and industrialization. More people worked in factories than ever before. People were proud of their country and of their military. Military **strategists** believed that if war did break out, it would be over quickly.

By 1914, disagreements between the Great Powers had reached a dangerous point. A single event would set off one of the most destructive wars in history. It was an assassin's bullet, and it became known as the "shot heard 'round the world."

> " The lamps are going out all over Europe; we shall not see them lit again in our lifetime.
>
> **SIR EDWARD GREY, ON THE EVE OF BRITAIN'S DECLARATION OF WAR** "

BELOW: *Families and well-wishers line the dock and wave good-bye to Australian troops as they leave to serve in the war.*

BUILDING STRONGER EMPIRES

Before the war, the five major European powers controlled huge areas of land across the globe. Great Britain had **colonies** around the world. Britain used its Royal Navy to ensure the safety of the trade routes between the British Empire's outposts. France had large colonies on the west and east coasts of Africa. The German Empire wanted to increase its overseas colonies by expanding small outposts in southern Africa. Russia hoped to expand into lands once controlled by the weakening Ottoman Empire.

Before the start of World War I, Europe was divided into two main **blocs**. The Allied Powers included the Triple Entente of Russia, France, and Britain. The Central Powers included the Triple Alliance of Germany, Austria-Hungary, and Italy. The Ottoman Empire was in decline. It was losing control of its provinces in southern Europe. There were also serious problems between the Austro-Hungarian Empire and the Russian Empire. The two were competing for territories in the **Balkans** that the Ottomans could no longer control.

WHAT DO YOU THINK?

Why was a strong navy important to the British Empire?

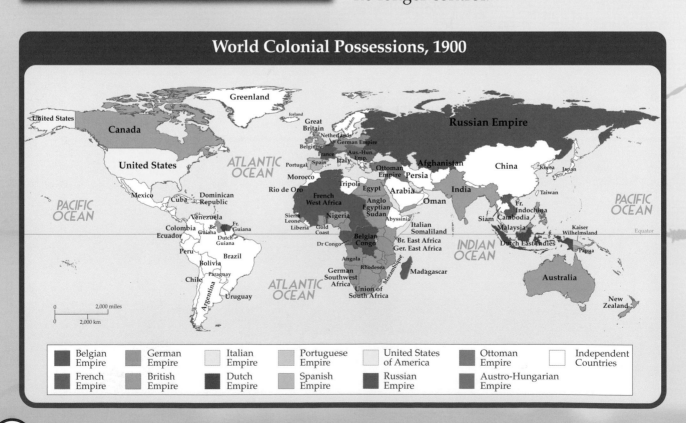

World Colonial Possessions, 1900

Legend:
- Belgian Empire
- French Empire
- German Empire
- British Empire
- Italian Empire
- Dutch Empire
- Portuguese Empire
- Spanish Empire
- United States of America
- Russian Empire
- Ottoman Empire
- Austro-Hungarian Empire
- Independent Countries

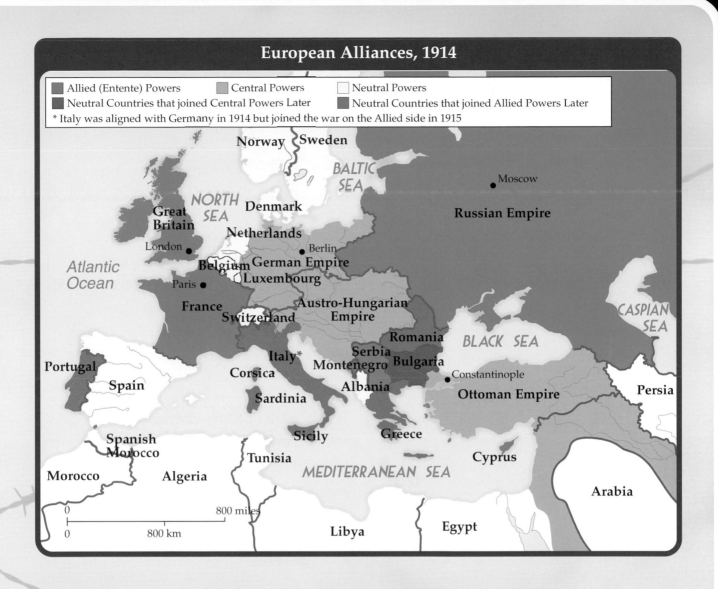

European Alliances, 1914

- ■ Allied (Entente) Powers
- ■ Central Powers
- □ Neutral Powers
- ■ Neutral Countries that joined Central Powers Later
- ■ Neutral Countries that joined Allied Powers Later

* Italy was aligned with Germany in 1914 but joined the war on the Allied side in 1915

Norway · Sweden · BALTIC SEA · Moscow · Russian Empire · NORTH SEA · Denmark · Great Britain · Netherlands · London · Berlin · Atlantic Ocean · Belgium · German Empire · Luxembourg · Paris · France · Austro-Hungarian Empire · Switzerland · CASPIAN SEA · Romania · BLACK SEA · Italy* · Serbia · Bulgaria · Portugal · Corsica · Montenegro · Constantinople · Persia · Spain · Albania · Ottoman Empire · Sardinia · Spanish Morocco · Sicily · Greece · Cyprus · Morocco · Algeria · Tunisia · MEDITERRANEAN SEA · Arabia · Libya · Egypt

0 — 800 miles
0 — 800 km

EUROPEAN POWERS BEFORE WORLD WAR I

In 1914, the Central Powers included three empires known as the Triple Alliance (see map above): the German Empire, the Austro-Hungarian Empire, and the Ottoman Empire. At the time, Italy and Bulgaria were also aligned with the Central Powers, although Italy would join the war on the Allied side instead in 1915.

At the start of the war, the Allied Powers included the British, French, and Russian empires—together called the Triple Entente—as well as Belgium, Japan, Serbia, Greece, Montenegro, and Romania. As the war progressed more countries were persuaded to join the Allied side.

CHAPTER 1

A CHANGING EUROPE

The years leading up to World War I were years of great change. The countries of Europe were growing closer through trade and commerce. New inventions such as the telegraph meant people could communicate across Europe more easily. Better railways and steamships made travel to foreign countries more affordable. The five great European powers had more contact with each other. Economic, political, and social ties were being created and contested. Conflicts arose as each power tried to protect its land and expand its resources.

ABOVE: *Czar Nicholas II of Russia (left) and his cousin King George V of England (right)*

THE BRITISH EMPIRE

Great Britain was the world's largest empire at the time. Its colonies stretched from Europe to North America, Asia, Africa, and Australia. Goods from the colonies were moved along trade routes. These goods included wheat from Canada, textiles from India, gold from South Africa, rubber from Malaysia, and sheep from Australia. British merchant ships relied on the Royal Navy for protection.

Britain's empire was growing larger. As the empire grew, control over the colonies and trade routes became more difficult. In 1898, Britain clashed with France over trade routes in Africa. France held land on the west and east coasts of Africa. Britain controlled

Egypt in the north and South Africa in the south. The trade routes used by both nations crossed near Fashoda in Sudan. Conflict was **inevitable**. France's small military force was met by British gunboats on the White Nile River. The French felt outnumbered and they retreated. Dutch settlers in South Africa called the Boers rose up against the British one year later. Britain was forced into what became a long and bitter struggle to defeat the Boers. This conflict worried Britain. It began to look for **allies** to strengthen and protect its empire.

BELOW: *Ships like this one carried freight from New Zealand to Britain.*

WHAT DO YOU KNOW?

ROYAL EUROPEAN DYNASTIES
In May 1910, Britain's King Edward VII died. Leaders from countries around the world traveled to London to attend his funeral. At the front of the procession were members of his family. The mourners included the **monarchs** of three of the world's greatest empires. Edward's son, Britain's new King George V, Russia's Czar Nicholas II, and Germany's Kaiser Wilhelm II were all cousins. When war loomed just a few years later, Kaiser Wilhelm said that if their grandmother Queen Victoria of England had been alive, she never would have allowed them to go to war with each other.

THE FRENCH REPUBLIC AND THE GERMAN EMPIRE

The Franco-Prussian War

France's government was different from other European powers of the time. The country did not have a king. It was a **republic**. France had been one of the largest and most powerful countries in Europe, and it was concerned about its neighboring countries. Prussia was to

KAISER WILHELM II (1859–1941)

Wilhelm II of Prussia was the last ruler of the German Empire. He was the eldest grandson of Queen Victoria of England. He was not considered a good leader because he sometimes made rash, or quick and not well-thought-out decisions. After the war, he **abdicated** and fled to Netherlands.

the east. (Prussia would later become part of Germany.) Spain lay to the south. In 1869, Prussia began to make connections with Spain. If a Prussian prince were to become king of Spain, France would be surrounded by large, powerful enemies. France wanted to prevent this from happening. Therefore, France declared war on Prussia in 1870. Only one year later, France's capital city Paris was surrounded. Its people were starving. The French surrendered. They were then forced to give the border province of Alsace-Lorraine to the new German Empire. The French never forgot the humiliation they suffered or the territory they lost in the Franco-Prussian War. The country felt an "esprit de revanche," or a desire for revenge, against Germany. This feeling lasted right up to the start of World War I.

The German Empire

In the mid-1800s, the area now known as Germany was not one country. It was made up of many small kingdoms, including Prussia. In 1871, these separate areas all joined together to form the German Empire. Kaiser Wilhelm I became king of the empire.

This new Germany quickly became more powerful. Factories produced high-quality steel. Railways were built. German scientists became leaders in research. In 1888, Kaiser Wilhelm I died, and Germany's new leader was Kaiser Wilhelm II. The new kaiser was far more **ambitious**. He wanted the German Empire to be larger and stronger than the French and British empires. Germany settled new colonies in Africa, East Asia, and the Pacific. Wilhelm II also wanted the German navy to be as powerful as the British navy. He built bigger and faster ships. Wilhelm II looked forward to the 20th century, with the goal of turning Germany into a great world power.

BELOW: *This ornate helmet made of leather and adorned with brass was the standard head gear for German troops when World War I began.*

BELOW: *Marianne, on this gold coin, is the national emblem of France and an important symbol of the French Republic. She stands for Liberty and reason and is the symbol of triumph for the French Republic.*

ABOVE: *The Krupp factory in Germany produced most of the steel, artillery, and ammunition used by the German army in World War I.*

THE RUSSIAN AND AUSTRO-HUNGARIAN EMPIRES

In 1894, Nicholas II became **czar**. He ruled the large and powerful Russian Empire. At one point, the empire stretched from Eastern Europe, across Asia, and into North America. Most of the population in this vast empire had worked as **serfs** on landowner's farms. It was a hard and poor life. During his reign, Czar Alexander II had worried that the 23 million serfs would **revolt**.

He began to free them in 1861. Many of the freed serfs and other Russians moved to the cities to work in new factories.

In 1904, the Russian Empire tried to expand into Northeast China and Korea. The Japanese wanted control of Korea, as well. This led to war between Russia and Japan. In the end, Japan defeated Russia. This was the first time an Asian nation had defeated a European nation. The Russian Empire faced threats from outside and inside its borders. A few years after the defeat by Japan, the Russian people began to revolt.

WHAT DO YOU THINK?
What events led European nations to think that the Russian Empire was weakening?

BELOW: *Before World War I, soldiers on horseback were enemies to be feared. The arms used in World War I, however, made cavalry troops ineffective.*

They were upset over terrible living conditions, low wages, and dangerous factory jobs in the cities. Many European nations saw that the Russian Empire was becoming weak.

In 1867, the nations of Austria and Hungary combined. They formed the Austro-Hungarian Empire. It was a dual monarchy. Austria and Hungary were separate states, but they shared finances, defense, and foreign affairs. It was unusual because both countries kept their own prime ministers and parliaments. Emperor Franz Joseph I ruled the empire. He was emperor of Austria and king of Hungary. He controlled the military and foreign policies for both nations. There were three armies in the empire: one from Austria, one from Hungary, and the Imperial Army. The soldiers in each of the armies spoke different languages. As a result, they often had trouble working together. Emperor Franz Joseph spent much of his time trying to maintain stability in the new empire.

Like the other great powers, Franz Joseph wanted to expand into new territory. The Balkan region stretched from the Balkan Mountains to the Mediterranean Sea. It was important land. The Balkans had miles of coastline for ports. It was ruled by the Turkish Ottoman Empire, but the Ottoman Empire was weakening. Both Austria-Hungary and Russia wanted to expand into the Balkan states, or at least keep each other out.

> "I do not see how anyone who sees his dearest relations leaving for the front can love war.
>
> **KAISER KARL OF AUSTRIA, ON THE OUTBREAK OF WORLD WAR I. KAISER KARL BECAME AUSTRO-HUNGARIAN RULER IN 1916, AFTER THE DEATH OF HIS GREAT-UNCLE EMPEROR FRANZ JOSEPH I.**"

RIGHT: *Emperor Franz Joseph I, ruler of the Austro-Hungarian empire*

The Sick Man of Europe

While it had once been a great power in Central Europe and the Middle East, by the 20th century, the Ottoman Empire was on the decline. It was frequently called "the sick man of Europe" as its power weakened.

The Ottoman Empire had existed for almost 600 years, having been founded by Turkish warriors toward the end of the 14th century. The Ottoman Empire was an **Islamic** state, which meant that the official religion of the state was Islam. At their height, the Ottomans were one of the most powerful forces in Central Europe and the Eastern Mediterranean. Their empire stretched across Turkey, parts of North Africa and Egypt, the Arabian Peninsula, Iraq, Syria, Palestine, and large portions of Ukraine and the Balkans. In 1529, Ottoman armies made it as far as the great Austrian city of Vienna.

By the 20th century, however, Ottoman control had been reduced to Turkey, Syria, Palestine, portions of Mesopotamia and the Arabian Peninsula, and some parts of the Balkans. Spreading **nationalism** had led many Balkan states to begin seeking independence in the later part of the 1800s.

In 1909, the **sultan** was deposed by a group of military officers calling themselves the Young Turks. The Young

ABOVE: *Ismail Enver Pasha, general and commander-in-chief of the Ottoman forces*

Turks, led by Enver Pasha, wanted to create a more centralized government and modernize the empire. A great railway was built connecting Berlin and Baghdad, but the Ottomans also developed trade relations with France and Britain. They also wanted to create a more **secular** state. Still, their losses of territory continued in the years leading up to World War I.

As war loomed on the horizon, the Ottomans wanted allies of their own. It was not immediately clear, however, which way they would turn if war broke out. Britain hoped the Turks would remain neutral. The Germans made many efforts to get the Ottomans to ally with them. Conflicts with Russia continued during those years, helping to influence Ottoman attitudes regarding what they would do in the event of war. In the end, the Ottomans agreed to an alliance with Germany, which they secretly signed in August of 1914. They hoped that a strong ally would help prevent further loss of territory when war broke out.

BELOW: *The three emperors of the Central Powers (left to right): Sultan Medmed V of Turkey, Kaiser Wilhelm II of Germany, and Emperor Franz Joseph of Austria-Hungary*

CHAPTER 2

PREPARING FOR WAR

The 19th century was a time of great change in the lives of working people. Most people's lives had been based on farming. They lived in rural areas and produced their own food. They also made their own clothing and furniture. The Industrial Revolution changed all that.

INDUSTRY AND THE EUROPEAN POWERS

The term *Industrial Revolution* refers to the change from an economy based mostly on farming to an economy based on manufacturing. New factories began to appear. They made fabric, chemicals, and steel. Manufacturers began to sell goods such as clothing, glass, soap, and even railway locomotives and steam ships. People no longer had to make the goods they needed to live. They could buy these things in stores. Thousands of workers left farm life for jobs that paid money. These jobs were in cities. Factories needed workers, and the workers came.

Natural resources, such as coal and iron ore, came from huge mines. Other raw materials, such as silk and cotton, came from overseas colonies. The European empires relied on their colonies to provide their factories with these raw materials. All the European powers scrambled to claim new colonies and to protect old ones. They needed safe ports and shipping routes to keep the raw materials flowing.

Britain was the first country to industrialize. It was known as "the workshop of the world."

LEFT: *Cotton to make these pillows came from overseas colonies.*

Other European countries hurried to keep up. They soon industrialized, too. German manufacturing advanced rapidly. Germany quickly led Europe in producing chemicals and steel. Both of these materials are essential parts for making weapons and **ammunition**. Germany was able to develop weapons, supplies, and equipment very quickly. This was one of the reasons why Germany was able to defeat France in the Franco-Prussian War. By 1913, Germany was producing more than Britain. This concerned Britain, France, and Russia. They knew that a country that could develop and move items quickly would be a huge threat if a war ever started.

BELOW: *These children are working during the Industrial Revolution, at a mill making stockings. Some children had to work at other jobs that were hard and dangerous.*

TRIPLE ALLIANCE

Otto von Bismarck was a **statesman** in Prussia. He played a major role in uniting the German states in 1871. Bismarck wanted to protect the new country. He believed the best way to do this was to make sure all the European countries had an equal amount of power. Most countries went to war because they believed they were stronger than their enemy. Bismarck believed that by keeping a "balance-of-power" there would be peace in Europe.

BELOW: *This handkerchief, showing Kings William I, Franz Josef, and Umberto I, celebrates the signing of the Triple Alliance on May 20, 1882.*

Bismarck believed that France posed the greatest threat to Germany. He knew France was still angry about losing the Alsace-Lorraine region in the Franco-Prussian War. Bismarck worried that France would become an ally of Russia. This would cause a problem if Germany were attacked because it would have to fight a war on two **fronts** at the same time. Germany's army would have to fight France in the west and Russia in the east. Bismarck believed Germany would lose the fight if this happened.

Bismarck wanted to strengthen Germany's position. To do this, he formed an alliance with Austria-Hungary. An alliance is an agreement between groups that have the same goals or the same interests. Germany and Austria-Hungary formed the Dual Alliance in 1879. They promised to help each other in case either country was attacked.

France removed its troops from Rome during the Franco-Prussian War. After the war, Italy became a united land. Its political situation gained stability. Its military gained strength and power. Italy then became involved in an argument with France over a colony in North Africa. In 1882, Italy joined with Germany and Austria-Hungary. Italy hoped the alliance would give it more power and help settle the **dispute**. This agreement among Germany, Austria-Hungary, and Italy was called the Triple Alliance. It would become very important in the days leading up to the start of World War I.

OTTO VON BISMARCK
(1815–1898)

Otto von Bismarck was a Prussian statesman who worked hard to unite the many separate German-speaking states into a single German empire. In 1862, he made a famous speech where he said the great questions concerning Prussia's future would not be solved by speeches but by "iron and blood," in other words, by military power. This earned him the nickname "Iron Chancellor." In 1890, Kaiser Wilhelm II, who was much more ambitious, removed him from office. Bismarck said, *"the crash will come twenty years after my departure if things go on like this."* World War I began 24 years later.

ABOVE: *The finance ministers of Britain, France, and Russia discuss the Triple Entente.*

TRIPLE ENTENTE

The formation of the Triple Alliance between Germany, Austria-Hungary, and Italy made other countries in Europe very nervous. They did not want these countries to become too powerful. The other empires began to form agreements of their own.

France and Russia paid attention when Germany, Italy, and Austria-Hungary joined forces. In 1894, France and Russia secretly formed the Dual Alliance. France had enemies all along its eastern border. It knew that it could not defeat Germany alone. France also knew that the situation would be much more difficult for Germany if France and Russia attacked at the same time. Germany would be forced to split its army. It would have to fight on both eastern and western fronts at the same time. France hoped that having Russia's support would help it win a war if the country were attacked.

In 1904, Britain and France entered into an **entente**. It was called the Entente Cordiale, or "friendly understanding." An entente was not as strong as an alliance. In an alliance, countries agreed to go to war for each other. In an entente, the countries promised to support each other if war broke out. Britain and France had been enemies for hundreds of years. However, the threat of the Triple Alliance brought them together. The Entente Cordiale settled their arguments over land in Africa and Newfoundland. In 1907, the Anglo-Russian Entente was signed. It sorted out land disputes in Asia between Russia and Britain. With that agreement, Britain, France, and Russia were locked together with a promise to support each other. This agreement became known as the Triple Entente.

Europe was now divided into two large blocs: the Triple Alliance and the Triple Entente. If a dispute broke out, no country would fight alone. Their allies would be called on to help. This set the stage for a much bigger conflict than had ever been seen before.

WHAT DO YOU KNOW?

THE GREAT GAME

Before they entered the Triple Entente, the British and Russian empires were enemies. They were locked in a battle for territory in Asia. This conflict, which had lasted almost 100 years, was called the Great Game. Britain and Russia fought over Afghanistan, and parts of China, Mongolia, and Tibet. Britain feared Russia was trying to gain territory to eventually attack British-held India. As the German Empire grew in power, the British and Russian empires finally put aside their differences. They became allies to **counter** the alliance between Germany and Austria-Hungary.

LEFT: *The Germans used posters, such as this one showing German soldiers dressed up as soldiers from France, Russia, and Britain, to frighten German citizens into joining the war effort.*

NAVAL RACE

Britain's Royal Navy was the largest and most powerful in the world at that time. It ruled the seas from the 16th century until the middle of the 20th century. The navy protected Britain's colonies and its trade routes. The government wanted to make sure that the Royal Navy stayed the most powerful in the world. To do this, they created the "Two-Power Standard." This policy meant that the British navy would always be bigger than the next two largest navies combined. In the early 1900s, these were the navies of Germany and Russia.

Kaiser Wilhelm II wanted to make Germany into a global empire. From the time he was a small boy, he had admired British naval ships and their power. Wilhelm wrote about this in his **autobiography**. He said that he wished someday to "possess as fine a navy as the English." Grand Admiral Alfred von Tirpitz was the head of Germany's Imperial Navy. He supported building large battleships. These ships would be able to compete directly with the British. The German navy began to build more and more ships, and the naval race was on.

BELOW: *One of the five twin-gun turrets, or towers, on the British warship HMS Dreadnought*

ABOVE: *A fleet of British dreadnoughts takes to the seas.*

In 1906, the nature of the race changed. Admiral Sir John "Jacky" Fisher, First Sea Lord of the British Navy, introduced a brand new kind of warship. The first one was called the **HMS** *Dreadnought*. Ships built before 1906 had a single main **battery** of large guns and many smaller guns. HMS *Dreadnought* was armed only with large 12-inch (305-mm) guns and was powered by steam turbines. It became the fastest and most powerful warship afloat. Every warship built after it was modeled on this design and known as a dreadnought.

Soon the race turned into a contest to see which country could build new dreadnoughts the fastest. Both the German and British people urged their governments to build more ships. By 1914, the British had 29 dreadnoughts and 9 dreadnought battle cruisers. Germany had 17 dreadnoughts and 7 dreadnought battle cruisers. At the start of the war, Britain still possessed the most powerful navy in the world.

WHAT DO YOU THINK?
Why were the dreadnought ships so important to the naval race?

23

CHAPTER 3

NATIONALISM AND MILITARISM

Nationalism is the belief in your own country's greatness and strength. Across Europe, people celebrated their culture and identity.

Governments, media, books, stories, and plays encouraged and supported this. National pride led each country to think that its government was right and strong. Each country and its citizens believed that their own nation would triumph in any conflict with any other nation.

NATIONALISM GROWS

Germany had won the Franco-Prussian war and was now unified. The German people knew their empire was very powerful. They had the largest steel industry in Europe. This helped them to make weapons, railroads, and vehicles quickly. The German people were proud of their strong economy and powerful military.

The German Empire had one culture. The Austro-Hungarian Empire spanned many regions. People from different areas had different backgrounds, languages, and religions. This caused problems for the Dual Monarchy. Some regions wanted independence. Nationalism fed that desire. People living in different areas wanted their own countries, not to be part of a larger empire.

Die Wacht am Rhein.

Er blickt hinauf in Himmelsau
Da Heldenväter niederschau'n
Und schwört in stolzer Kampfeslust
Du Rhein bleibst deutsch wie meine Brust.
Lieb Vaterland :,:

ABOVE: *An inspirational, or encouraging, poster showing the title and one verse of the German patriotic song, "The Watch on the Rhine."*

ABOVE: *German soldiers leaving for the battlefront in August 1914*

Russia was a large empire, but it was **landlocked**. It needed land that was near a warm-water port. Russia was still humiliated from its defeat in the war with Japan. Russia needed to prove to the world that it was still strong. It intended to build its military and its global power. The country also felt great pride in its **Slavic** culture. It wanted to unite all the Slavic people. Some Slavic regions in the Balkans bordered the Mediterranean Sea. These regions were held by the Austro-Hungarian Empire. Russia could reach two of its goals—a warm-water port and **unification** of the Slavic people—if it had control of this area.

The French were still stinging from their defeat against the Prussians. Their national pride would not be healed until they took back the Alsace-Lorraine territory that was held by Germany.

WHAT DO YOU KNOW?

HAPPY TO GO TO WAR

Nationalism in Germany ran very high at the beginning of the war. The German public was confident they would win any war. As the soldiers left their homes, people smothered them with flowers and chocolates. They gave them so much that the Red Cross asked them to cut back. The soldiers ate so many sweets that they were getting sick!

Britain felt great national pride at the size and power of its empire. Britain had the most territory and the strongest navy in the world. It felt very secure. Then, other empires began building factories and expanding their industries. They were also adding territory. Britain knew it had to act fast to keep its world position and maintain control of its empire.

ABOVE: *Years before the war began, Germans were turning zeppelins into war machines.*

MILITARISM

The Great Powers of Europe knew that they needed to control and protect their expanding empires. They believed there was only one way to do this. They needed a strong, powerful military. Money and resources were used to build up armies and **defense systems**. Militarism, or belief in the need for a strong military force, changed the way leaders and civilians thought about war.

The Industrial Revolution increased the production and development of weapons. It also spread militarism. Factories produced huge numbers of guns and ammunition. New weapons also were developed. Artillery was developed that could shoot over large distances very accurately. The fully automatic machine gun was improved, too. It became smaller and lighter.

Building Military Forces

Before the buildup to World War I, most armies were made up of professional soldiers. But for World War I, countries looked to ordinary people to form their military forces. Some countries required most young men to train as soldiers. The military put on parades and demonstrations to show off their strength and skills.

In Russia, most 20-year-old males were expected to serve in the army. At first young men were drafted into service, then other men were taken into the

reserves. In Germany, young men had been called into the military for many years. About 60 percent of young men were called to serve when they were 20 years old and trained for two to three years. After that, they could return to civilian life. Most of the soldiers in the British and German armies came from industrial centers. Many French soldiers were farmers from the countryside. They were used to a hard, open-air lifestyle. This meant that French soldiers would be able to deal with life in the trenches better than other soldiers.

Many people believed war was coming. However, some people thought that a powerful military was not a step toward war. Instead, they believed that a military buildup of both men and machines would actually prevent wars.

WHAT DO YOU KNOW?
BIG BERTHA

Artillery weapons in World War I were large guns usually transported on wheels or rail cars. These large guns caused more destruction in World War I than any other type of weapon. Artillery weapons could fire very large explosive **shells** at enemies a long distance away. One of the largest, a German gun nicknamed "Big Bertha," could fire a 2,100-pound (953 kg) shell from about 9 miles (14.5 km) away. The gun and its carriage weighed about 75 tons (68 tonnes).

They thought that no one would dare attack a country with advanced weapons and huge armies. If a war did break out, they believed their strong military meant that it would end very quickly.

LEFT: *German troops set up Big Bertha, a massive artillery gun.*

PLANS FOR WAR

Long before the start of World War I, the major European powers were developing war plans. The chief of the Great German General Staff was Count Alfred von Schlieffen. He knew that Germany would likely face enemies in the east (Russia) and the west (France). He did not want to split his army to fight on two fronts. He developed what was known as the Schlieffen Plan.

His plan was to attack and defeat France first. This would be done before Russia had a chance to put its army into position. He knew that France had built a line of protective forts along its border with Germany. They had been put up to prevent an attack from the Germans. Schlieffen figured out that the only way to attack France quickly was to go north around the forts. According to the plan, Germany would go through Belgium and Luxembourg. These two were **neutral countries**. German forces would then move south into France and surround Paris. There, the Germans would trap the French army and force it to surrender. After that occurred, German troops could move back across Germany to prepare for the fight against Russia.

In France, Marshal Joseph Joffre was also making war plans for his country. Joffre knew that the smaller French army would have to respond quickly if

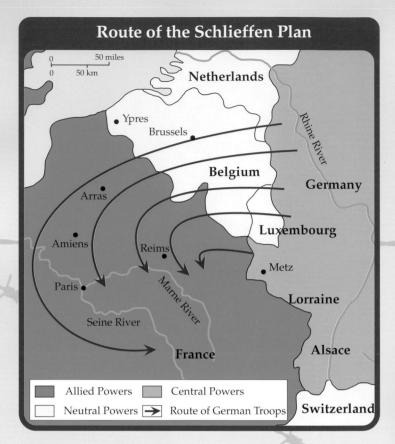

Route of the Schlieffen Plan

Netherlands
Ypres
Brussels
Belgium
Rhine River
Germany
Arras
Luxembourg
Amiens
Reims
Metz
Paris
Marne River
Lorraine
Seine River
France
Alsace

- Allied Powers
- Central Powers
- Neutral Powers
- → Route of German Troops

Switzerland

WHAT DO YOU KNOW?

NEUTRAL COUNTRIES

A country that is neutral has declared that it will not take sides nor fight in a war. Neutral countries have rights and duties. Countries at war may not invade neutral territory. Any troops who are found there are held by the neutral country. Warring countries cannot **recruit** troops from a neutral country. They also cannot move people or supplies across neutral land, but they may move the wounded. Even ships can only stay in a neutral port long enough to make repairs.

Germany attacked. His plan was named Plan XVII. It called for an immediate **offensive** attack across the border, directly at the enemy. He did not think that Germany would cross the Belgian border.

The German and French plans each had flaws. Joffre's plan assumed that Germany would never attack from the north. Joffre did not believe that the Germans would dare cross through a neutral country. The French believed that Britain would protect Belgium. Britain's protection would prevent Germany from crossing through the neutral country. Joffre was mistaken.

The Schlieffen Plan called for the German army to cross through neutral Belgium and attack France from its northern border, as well as from the east. For the plan to work, Germany had to defeat France quickly. The Germans had to finish fighting in the west before the Russians were ready for battle in the east. If the German army was delayed in France, or could not get troops quickly enough to the eastern front, the plan could fall apart.

Nations on each side felt protected by the alliances they had made. The Great Powers of Europe may have believed that their plans would actually prevent war from breaking out. In fact, by creating these plans, they were preparing for war.

ALFRED VON SCHLIEFFEN (1833–1913)

Count Alfred von Schlieffen, the son of a Prussian general, joined the army in 1854. He participated in the Seven Weeks' War with Austria in 1866 and in the Franco-Prussian War in 1870–1871. He then served as chief of the Imperial Army's general staff from 1891 through 1905. He retired from the military in 1906. He is best known for his 1905 military plan to defeat France and then move troops to battle on the Eastern Front. The plan was put into action in 1914 during World War I and again during World War II.

CHAPTER 4

CLOSE CALLS TO WAR

CRISIS IN MOROCCO

Morocco is a country in northeast Africa. France controlled most of Morocco and was interested in colonizing it. French interests were supported by Britain. Their growing partnership concerned Germany.

Under the Entente Cordiale, France recognized Britain's control over Egypt. Britain recognized France's interests in Morocco. Germany did not like this development. It was worried that Britain and France were becoming a powerful threat since they joined forces.

Germany wanted to keep some control over Morocco and to drive Britain and France apart. It used developments in Morocco to try to achieve this goal. On March 31, 1905, Kaiser Wilhelm II of Germany went to Morocco and met with the sultan. Wilhelm said he supported an independent Morocco, not one under French control. The sultan then requested a meeting with the major world powers to advise him.

France refused to attend the conference. The country had no intention of handing over control of Morocco.

BELOW: *The coast of Morocco, an African country controlled and protected by France during World War I*

Germany threatened war over the issue and began calling in reserve units. France moved its troops to the border with Germany. France was not willing to go to war, however, and eventually agreed to attend the meeting

At the conference, Germany hoped to get support from the other major powers. Only Austria-Hungary sided with Germany. France had the support of Britain and Russia. It also had the support of other countries including Italy, Spain, and the United States. Germany had failed to divide Britain and France. If anything, the two nations had developed stronger ties.

This issue bubbled up again in 1911. A rebellion broke out in Morocco against the sultan. France sent troops to put down the rebellion. Germany reacted by sending a gunboat. Britain raced to support France by threatening to send its own ships. Germany backed down, but the lines were clearly drawn as to who was siding with whom.

WHAT DO YOU KNOW?

THE STRAIT OF GIBRALTAR

The Strait of Gibraltar is a narrow waterway that connects the Atlantic Ocean and the Mediterranean Sea. It is also known as the Pillars of Hercules. On the north side are Spain and Gibraltar, which is a territory of Britain. On the south side is Morocco. By controlling Morocco, France would have some control over this important shipping route.

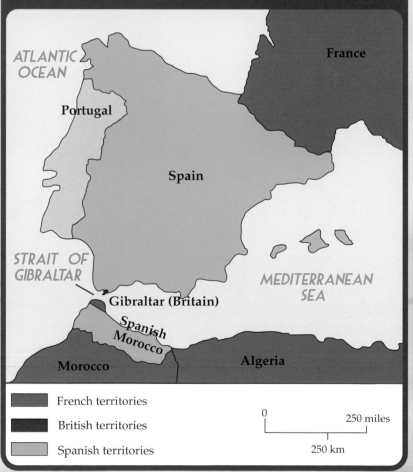

The Strait of Gibraltar
French troops were stationed in Morocco so that the French could protect their territory.

ATLANTIC OCEAN

France

Portugal

Spain

STRAIT OF GIBRALTAR

Gibraltar (Britain)

Spanish Morocco

MEDITERRANEAN SEA

Morocco

Algeria

French territories
British territories
Spanish territories

0   250 miles

250 km

THE BALKAN CRISIS

Tensions were high after the Moroccan crisis. The major European powers were still fighting for territory and testing their new alliances. The Balkan states were the next battleground.

The Balkan Peninsula juts out into the Mediterranean Sea. It had been controlled by the Ottoman Empire since the 1300s. Some of the Balkan states, such as Greece and Serbia, had become independent countries. Another large part of the Balkans, however, was still held by the Ottoman Empire. As the Ottoman Empire weakened, Austria-Hungary hoped to use that chance to expand its territory. In 1906, the Pig War broke out between Austria-Hungary and Serbia over trade relations between the two. In 1908, Austria-Hungary **annexed** the Slavic provinces of Bosnia and Herzegovina. This angered the Serbians who wanted the area to become part of "Greater Serbia." Russia, who saw itself as a protector of all Slavic people, supported Serbia. Austria-Hungary then turned to Germany for support.

ABOVE: *This image from a French newspaper depicts the leaders of Austria and Bulgaria taking territory away from the Ottoman (Turkish) Empire.*

Germany had a much more powerful army than Russia at the time. At the Treaty of Berlin in 1909, Russia and Serbia were forced to accept terms ending the conflict.

Outcome of the Balkan Wars

Austria-Hungary

Russia

Romania

Sarajevo

Belgrade ●

● Bucharest

Serbia

Montenegro

Bulgaria

Sofia ●

BLACK SEA

Albania

Constantinople ●

Italy

AEGEAN SEA

Ottoman Empire

Greece

Athens ●

IONIAN SEA

| 0 | | 200 miles |
| 0 | 200 km | |

——— Area controlled by the Ottoman Empire prior to 1912

///// Area lost by the Ottoman Empire during the Balkan Wars

——— International boundaries in 1913 following the Balkan Wars

Russia saw this as another military humiliation. It began to modernize its army more quickly. It was determined not to be embarrassed again.

After the Balkan crisis, Serbia, Bulgaria, Greece, and Montenegro formed the Balkan League. They had Russia's support. In 1912, they fought for independence in the First Balkan War against the Ottoman Empire. The Balkan League won and conquered Turkey's land in Europe. In 1913, the Balkan countries began fighting each other in the Second Balkan War. Serbia emerged as the most powerful state. It quickly set its sights on its earlier enemy, Austria-Hungary. Austria-Hungary was worried. The Balkan conflicts added to the heated tensions in Europe. The stage was being set for war.

WHAT DO YOU KNOW?

THE OTTOMAN EMPIRE

The Ottoman Empire was also called the Turkish Empire. It was one of the world's largest and longest-lasting empires. The empire's capital was Constantinople, which we now know as Istanbul, Turkey. For over 600 years, this empire controlled southeastern Europe, Northern Africa, and Western Asia. It almost completely surrounded the Mediterranean Sea and had a powerful navy. It began to weaken in the 1800s and, after World War I, it completely **dissolved**.

RIGHT: *Mustafa Kemal Atatürk fought for Turkey's independence and became the country's first president.*

THE WAR BEGINS

The Slavic people, called Slavs, living in Bosnia-Herzegovina saw Serbia's success. They wanted to send a message to Austria-Hungary that they would no longer be ruled by them. Some of the Slavs believed the only way to prove their point and achieve independence was to **assassinate** a high-ranking official.

SENDING A MESSAGE

Archduke Franz Ferdinand was the **heir** to the Austro-Hungarian Empire. On June 28, 1914, he and his wife Sophie were visiting Sarajevo in Bosnia. The couple planned to inspect the Imperial Army. They knew that visiting Bosnia was risky. There had been several assassination attempts against officials in the previous five years. June 28 was also the anniversary of an important Serbian victory. It was a date that might give the Bosnians a reason to rebel. The archduke decided to go anyway.

Learning of the royal couple's plans, a terrorist group called the Black Hand decided to target them. Bosnian-Serbs

ABOVE: *Archduke Franz Ferdinand and Sophie*

Gavrilo Princip, Trifko Grabez, and Nedeljko Cabrinovic were members of the Young Bosnia movement. They wanted to help the Black Hand bring about changes in Bosnia. These three were joined in the plot by Serbian youths in Sarajevo. All of them were supplied with weapons from the Black Hand. Each of the six carried bombs, a pistol, and a **cyanide** pill. They were supposed to commit suicide after the assassination.

Eyewitness: Borijove Jevtic, one of the Serbian conspirators of the assassination:

"[June 28] is a date engraved deeply in the heart of every Serb. . . . It is also the day on which in the second Balkan War the Serbian arms took glorious revenge on the Turk for his old victory and for the years of enslavement.

That was no day for Franz Ferdinand, the new **oppressor**, to venture to the very doors of Serbia for a display of the force of arms which kept us beneath his heel.

Our decision was taken almost immediately. Death to the tyrant!"

WHAT DO YOU THINK?

What did the assassins hope to achieve by killing Franz Ferdinand? Should the archduke have delayed his visit, considering how dangerous it was?

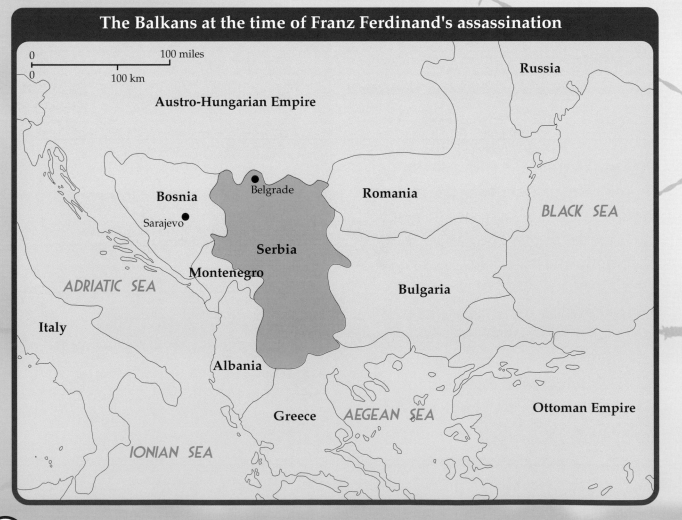

The Balkans at the time of Franz Ferdinand's assassination

0 — 100 miles
0 — 100 km

Russia

Austro-Hungarian Empire

Bosnia
Sarajevo

Belgrade

Romania

BLACK SEA

Serbia

Montenegro

ADRIATIC SEA

Bulgaria

Italy

Albania

Greece   AEGEAN SEA

Ottoman Empire

IONIAN SEA

ABOVE: *The assassination of Archduke Franz Ferdinand and his wife Sophie, June 28, 1914*

GAVRILO PRINCIP
(1894–1918)

Gavrilo Princip was born in Bosnia-Herzegovina. He was sick and frail as a child from **tuberculosis**. He went to elementary school in Bosnia but, at age 16, he moved to Serbia to continue his education. There he joined the Black Hand terrorist group. He knew his illness meant he would not live long. He wanted to do something meaningful with his life. He thought that the assassination would help bring independence for Bosnia. He died in prison four years later. He was hailed a hero by the Bosnian people.

THE ASSASSINATION

On June 28, the assassins lined the route that Franz Ferdinand and the other officials would take. Not worried about security, the royal couple was riding in a **convertible** with the top down. As the cars went by, Cabrinovic threw a bomb at the royal couple's car. It hit the back, rolled off, and exploded under the next car. An officer and a number of onlookers were wounded, but Franz Ferdinand was unharmed. Cabrinovic tried to commit suicide by swallowing the pill and jumping off a bridge into a river. The pill did not work, and the river was too shallow for hiding. Police dragged him out of the river and arrested him.

Franz Ferdinand was urged to leave Sarajevo. Instead, he decided to visit an officer who had been wounded in the attack. In the confusion that followed on the way to the hospital, the car carrying the archduke got lost. It happened to be near where Princip was standing. He took out his gun and shot Franz Ferdinand and Sophie at close range. They died on their way to the hospital.

After the shooting, Princip tried to raise his gun to shoot himself. The crowd around him grabbed his arm and stopped him. He was arrested and stood trial.

WAR BY TIMETABLE

Austria-Hungary was outraged that one of its officials had been murdered. The government had to act quickly. It needed to keep control of the area.

The Austro-Hungarian Empire could not let this event lead to Bosnia-Herzegovina's independence. They also could not afford to let Serbia become any stronger. Serbia and its supporter, Russia, were building up their military forces. Germany promised to support Austria-Hungary in a war against Serbia.

Austria-Hungary believed it would have to strike right away. The German and Austro-Hungarian people were demanding war. Austria-Hungary

ABOVE: *German soldiers called for duty from their reserve units depart from Berlin on their way to the Western Front in 1914.*

knew that the Serbian terrorist group the Black Hand was behind the plot. The country's leaders believed this gave them the excuse they needed to attack Serbia. If they waited, French and Russian armies would have more time to prepare and assemble their troops for war.

In the early 1900s, it was difficult to move troops quickly. Military leaders believed that the country that could move its troops the fastest would win any war. At the time, troops and supplies could be moved fastest by railroad. So military staff planned complicated train schedules. The timetables were extremely tight so that they could get their men and equipment to the front before their enemies arrived. Historians called this "War by Timetable."

Building railway tracks and railway cars became a major industry. Armies would have entire **regiments** of railroad engineers. Military powers also thought that having other countries know they had this ability would be enough to prevent war.

RIGHT: *German soldiers carrying weapons and equipment march along a road to Albert, France, a small town north of Paris.*

WHAT DO YOU KNOW?

A PORTABLE RAILWAY

The first portable railway track was made in 1795. In the 1800s, the British and French improved on the idea. Germans developed their own portable railway that could carry special tiny locomotives, flat cars, and sections of rail. Even little sections of bridges were loaded on and moved to the front. There, men could assemble a railroad, complete with small bridges over ravines, in a very short time behind their battle lines. Supplies, ammunition, and even wounded men could be moved quickly and easily. This kept their troops fed and armed. When the front shifted, they could disassemble the railway and send it to a new location.

ONE LAST CHANCE

Austria-Hungary sent a letter to Serbia on July 24. This document was called the July **Ultimatum**. It listed Austria-Hungary's demands and gave Serbia 48 hours to reply. The ultimatum was designed to make it impossible for Serbia to agree to the terms. In its response, Serbia did not accept two of Austria's demands. Serbia realized that it would soon be under attack. Serbia called on Russia for help. Russia had supported the Serbs during the Balkan crisis and stood ready to help again.

On July 28, 1914, Austria-Hungary declared war on Serbia. Russia began to mobilize troops in response. Austria-Hungary's alliance brought Germany into the conflict. Germany warned Russia to stop mobilizing, but Russia refused. Germany then declared war on Russia on August 1, 1914.

Now at war with Russia, Germany knew it would soon have problems with another member of Russia's Triple Entente: France. It sent France a letter, demanding a promise of neutrality. France refused and mobilized its army, but it did not attack Germany. Germany was following the Schlieffen Plan. Germany would try to defeat France first. Then it could move all its troops to the east to deal with Russia.

Germany declared war on France on August 3 and moved its forces into Belgium. It was going to attack France from its unprotected north. Belgium, still a neutral country, was protected by Britain. Britain sent an ultimatum to Germany to leave Belgium. Germany refused because it did not think Britain would go to war with the German Empire over such a small country.

Britain then declared war on Germany on August 4, 1914. Britain's empire at that time included Canada, Australia, and New Zealand. These countries were then also involved in the conflict because of their ties to Britain.

Only a month after the assassination of Franz Ferdinand, all the major powers of Europe, as well as several other countries, were at war.

Die Niederlage der Serben

ABOVE: *This painting, The Defeat of the Serbs, captures the fate and hardships faced by the soldiers.*

Events Leading to World War I

Date	Event	Summary
May 29, 1867	Austria-Hungary is formed.	Austro-Hungarian compromise creates Dual Monarchy.
July 19, 1870	Franco-Prussian War	Prussians defeat France and take control of Alsace-Lorraine.
January 18, 1871	Countries come together to form Germany.	Wilhelm I of Prussia is declared emperor of German Empire.
May 1882	Triple Alliance	Germany, Austria-Hungary, and Italy agree to fight for each other.
February 8, 1904	Russo-Japanese War	Russian and Japanese forces clash over territory. Russia is defeated, shocking other European nations.
March 1905	First Moroccan crisis	Germany tries to use Morocco's desire for independence to create friction between Britain and France.
August 1907	Triple Entente	Understanding to support each other between Britain, France, and Russia
July 1911	Second Moroccan crisis	French troops sent to Morocco to fight a revolt. Germany sends a gunboat, which upsets both France and Britain. Germany backs down, and France takes over Morocco.
October 8, 1912	First Balkan War	Serbia, Bulgaria, Greece, and Montenegro fight for independence from the Turkish Ottoman Empire. They succeed, and the war ends on May 30, 1913, with the Treaty of London.
June 29, 1913	Second Balkan War	Bulgaria turns on its former allies, Serbia and Greece, and is defeated by them. This ends the strong Balkan League. Austria-Hungary is concerned by how strong Serbia had grown.
June 28, 1914	Assassination of Franz Ferdinand	Archduke Franz Ferdinand and his wife Sophie are killed by Gavrilo Princip.
July 28, 1914	Austria-Hungary declares war on Serbia.	The assassination is used as an excuse to attack Serbia.
August 1, 1914	Germany declares war on Russia.	To protect Serbia, Russia mobilizes its army. This threatens Germany, which declares war on Russia. France mobilizes troops.
August 3, 1914	Germany declares war on France.	Using the Schlieffen Plan, Germany plans to defeat France quickly.
August 4, 1914	Britain declares war on Germany.	Britain declares war on Germany when Belgium is invaded.

THE MARCH TOWARD WAR

The cause of World War I is not found in one single event. It was the result of many small and some major changes in Europe. Weapons and transportation became faster and stronger. Military forces grew larger and more powerful. Countries made alliances with each other to protect their interests. Regions fought for independence from empires.

People's ways of thinking had changed, too. They developed pride in the size and strength of their nations. They supported the race to build bigger militaries. Each nation thought it could never be defeated.

Tensions that were building across Europe came to a boiling point in Sarajevo. The assassination of Franz Ferdinand set off a chain reaction. That single act changed the history and shape of Europe. War was declared. Countries not directly involved in the situation in Bosnia were called to honor their alliances. Soon all of the Great Powers of Europe were part of something unthinkable—the very first world war.

WHAT DO YOU THINK?
How would the war have been different without the Triple Alliance and the Triple Entente?

BELOW: *This German order for troops to assemble was signed by Kaiser Wilhelm II on August 1, 1914. By November, thousands of troops were on the Western Front. Here, German soldiers march through France.*

FURTHER READING AND WEBSITES

BOOKS

Carter, Miranda. *George, Nicholas and Wilhelm: Three Royal Cousins and the Road to World War I.* New York: Vintage Books, 2011.

Clark, Christopher. *The Sleepwalkers: How Europe Went to War in 1914.* New York: Harper, 2013.

Hastings, Max. *Catastrophe 1914: Europe Goes to War.* New York: Knopf, 2013.

Hemingway, Ernest. *A Farewell to Arms.* New York: Simon and Schuster, 1995.

King, Greg, and Sue Woolmans. *The Assassination of the Archduke: Sarajevo 1914 and the Romance That Changed the World.* New York: St. Martin's Press, 2013.

MacMillan, Margaret. *The War That Ended Peace: The Road to 1914.* New York: Random House, 2013.

Olender, Piotr. *Russo-Japanese Naval War 1905, Vol. 2 (Maritime Series).* Hampshire, UK: Mushroom Model Publishing, 2010.

Remarque, Erich Maria, and A.W. Wheen. *All Quiet on the Western Front.* New York: Fawcett Books, 1987.

Tuchman, Barbara W. *The Guns of August.* New York: Random House, 2003.

WEBSITES

The Origins of World War One
www.bbc.co.uk/history/ worldwars/wwone/origins_01.shtml

WWI Timeline: Pre-1914
www.pbs.org/greatwar/timeline

Europe at the Turn of the Century
www.inflandersfields.be/en/ world-war-i-in-flanders/time-line

The Willy-Nicky Telegrams
www.firstworldwar.com/source/ willynicky.htm

GLOSSARY

abdicated   to formally relinquish power or responsibility

alliances   formal associations of nations or groups

allies   groups that join with another or others out of mutual interest

ambitious   wanting to be successful, famous, or powerful

ammunition   projectiles that can be fired from a gun or otherwise propelled

annexed   absorbed another territory into a larger existing political unit

artillery   large caliber weapons, such as cannons, that are operated by crews

assassinate   to murder by surprise attack, often for political reasons

autobiography   the biography, or story of person's life, written by that person

Balkans   the easternmost of Europe's peninsulas, that includes the countries of modern-day Slovenia, Croatia, Bosnia and Herzegovina, Serbia, Kosovo, Montenegro, Macedonia, Albania, Bulgaria, Romania, and Moldova

battery   an emplacement for artillery; a set of heavy guns on a warship

blocs   group of nations, parties, or people united by common interest

colonies   distant territories that are controlled by or that belong to another country

convertible   automobile with a top that can be removed or folded back

counter   to move or act in opposition

cyanide   poisonous compound of potassium cyanide and sodium cyanide

czar   Russian ruler; a king

defense systems   means or methods of defending or protecting

dispute   an argument or conflict

dissolved   formally ended

entente   agreement between two or more governments or powers for cooperative action or policy

Factory Acts   series of laws in Great Britain regulating the operation of factories, designed to improve the working conditions of women and children

fronts   areas where military forces are fighting; the most forward lines of a combat force